Love At Our Roots   James H. Commander

Love At Our Roots   James H. Commander

Love At Our Roots   James H. Commander

"**As ye have therefore received Christ Jesus the Lord, walk ye in him: Rooted and built up in him, and stablished by the faith, as ye have been taught, abounding therein with thanksgiving.**"
-Colossians 2:6-2:7 [KJV]-

Love At Our Roots   James H. Commander

Love At Our Roots — James H. Commander

© COPYRIGHT March 11, 2010, James Commander

Love At Our Roots					James H. Commander

Love At Our Roots   James H. Commander

OTHER BOOKS BY JAMES H. COMMANDER

Excuse Me Ms!: An Anti-Male Bashing Handbook

Handle Your 'BITS'ness: An Approach to Niche Music Business Marketing

POETRY

SOUL Libations

SOULjourn: The Poetic Quests of Da Red AdmiRAW

SOUL Reign

AUDIO BOOKS

SOULjourn: The Poetic Quests of Da Red AdmiRAW

Chocoletta: The Accapella Album

SOUL 7 I AMZ

Love At Our Roots   James H. Commander

Love At Our Roots　　　　　　　　　　　James H. Commander

LOVE
at our
ROOTS.

© COPYRIGHT March 11, 2010, James Commander

HOW FREEDOM BECAME A FORCE FOR CHANGE.

MR. JAMES H. COMMANDER

Love At Our Roots   James H. Commander

Love At Our Roots   James H. Commander

Love At Our Roots   James H. Commander

The MO Amper, LLC
COPYRIGHT © JAMES H. COMMANDER, 2013
© (p) The MO Amper, LLC, Audio Book Excerpt/Poetry LP
All rights reserved.

Printed in the United States of America
Designed by James H. Commander
About the Author photo by Rosemerry Felder-Commander

The MO Amper, LLC. And its subsidiaries The MO Amper Sounds Publishing
www.moamper.com

All images from collection of James H. Commander except the following: Pg. 32- Henry Spaulding (1926 Chicago Normal yearbook);Pg 49 – Mary Bethune & Maida Kemp (unknown photographer); pp. 38-39 (Kemp, Marjorie. Letter from Marjorie Kemp to W. E. B. Du Bois, ca. May 1931. W. E. B. Du Bois Papers (MS 312). Special Collections and University Archives, University of Massachusetts Amherst Libraries); pg. 40 – Good Shepherd basement 1940 (unknown photographer); Pg. 50 James & Maida Kemp; A. Philip Randolph(photo by Ed Jackson Studio); Pg. 60 Betty Everett & James Kemp (photo excerpt from Jet 1963) Pg. 98 #105 James H. Kemp RTA Train (photographer unknown)

Without limiting the rights under copyright above, no part of this publication may be reproduced, stored in or introduced into retrieval system, or transmitted, in any form or by any means (electronic, mechanical, photocopying, recording or otherwise), without the prior written permission of both the copyright owner and the above publisher of this book.

The scanning, uploading, and distribution of this book via the internet or via any other means without the permission of the publisher is illegal and punishable by law. Please purchase only authorized electronic editions and do not participate in or encourage electronic piracy of copyrightable materials. You support of the author's rights is appreciated.

Library of Congress Cataloging-in-Publication Data
Love at Our Roots: How Freedom Became A Force For Change. / Edited and Authored by James H. Commander.
      1. American / African American History   2. Genealogy

Library of Congress Control Number: 2013910955
ISBN: 9780989564915 (Print-Paperback)
ISBN: 9780989564908 (E-book)

10 9 8 7 6 5 4

First Edition

Love At Our Roots					James H. Commander

Love At Our Roots   James H. Commander

In Loving Memory & Dedication:

Cicero, Aria, Anaca, Louis, Marjorie, Julia, Juanita, Aleene, Celestine, Julia, Joseph, Ethel, James Sr., Sadie Lee, James Jr. & Maida Kemp

Henry Spaulding & Novella Smith

The Most Hon. Elijah Muhammad (PBUH)
Sister Clara & Jabir (Herbert) Muhammad (PBUH)

~

In Loving Guidance:

ALL
nieces,
nephews,
great-nieces,
great-nephews,
children, grandchildren
and the future generations -
Royce (a son of the King) and
Rayna (princess & lioness) may you
adhere, maintain, and evolve in this legacy.

Special Thanks & Dedication:

<u>My Three Mothers</u>
Mama Pamela Spaulding-Commander
(Rest-in-Peace)
Mama Mildred Whitlock-Johnson
Mama Jerline "twin" Shelton

<u>My "Kindred-Soul" Relative</u>
Francis Taylor-Dunham-Catlett

~

ALL well-wishing family members:
Kemp
Spaulding
Jefferies
Smith
Muhammad
Commander
Hicks-Hood-Harris
Blackman
Shelton
Brandy
Whitlock
Johnson
Carwise
Felder
Burnside
Goodine
Freeman

A special expression of thanks to **Elizabeth (Betty) Thomas** of the Charlotte School of Law library staff for providing information for the Family Search genealogical research data bases of the Jesus Christ of Latter Day Saints (Mormons). The resource proved to be an invaluable complement to the researching tools of the Ancestry.com database.

Additional moral support, encouragement, genealogical resources and historical reference books about the "four great migrations" were provided by one of the remaining family matriarchs—our great cousin **Beverly Kemp-Helm**. Your oral accounts of family history, zeal, and passion for uncovering hidden historical treasures contagiously inspires me.

An ever grateful thanks to the expert assistance of librarians and staff from the Vivian G. Harsh Research Library in Chicago, Columbia College of Chicago, the Hyde Park Historical Society in Chicago, **Juliette Smith** and **Linda Edmunds** of Talladega College, and the staff at the Alabama Department of Archives and History in Montgomery, Alabama.

Last—but never least—a heartfelt thank you to **Ms. Ruth A. Mazique**, **Rev. Jesse Knox III**, and the **"family" at the Church of the Good Shepherd Congregational United Church of Christ** in Chicago, Illinois. May the "light of faith" show the path for another century of service.

Contents

Introduction

Chapter One
A Patch of Blue
1

Chapter Two
A Miracle of The Good Shepherd
17

Chapter Three
Staggered Not at The Promise
42

Chapter Four
Endure All Things
51

Chapter Five
To Whom Much Is Given
85

Epilogue
103

Notes
115

About The Author
122

INTRODUCTION

"Either what woman having ten pieces of silver, if she lose one piece, doth not light a candle, and sweep the house, and seek diligently till she find it?
And when she hath found it, she calleth her friends and her neighbours together, saying, Rejoice with me; for I have found the piece which I had lost."
-Luke 15:8-9 [KJV]

LOVE—the fruit of which is regeneration as well as multiplication—that is the power at the root of this writing (A love to, for, from, and about self by way of discovery, reflection, and a vision for the future).

A pivotal life occurrence, from which LOVE found expression, as it is relevant to this literary undertaking, exists in the memories of my early childhood. During a conversation among four other siblings about *inheritance*, WHILE IN HER PRESENCE, the words to my Great Aunt Juanita Kemp was that she did not have to give me ANY material thing upon her death—because she had taken me from an impoverished condition and given me food, clothing, shelter and LOVE. Immediately, upon hearing my sentiments, she was moved to tears and later made sure to tell all of her friends about my declaration.

It is from that source of love that the title of this book springs forth because it is from her selfless act of love that my personal and ancestral roots are incessantly nourished.

Hopefully some of the love will provide inspiration during the quest to nurture your roots.

Warm Regards,

James H. Commander

CHAPTER 1

A PATCH OF BLUE
1889 - 1922

"It is a gray day."
"Yes, but dinna ye see the patch of blue?"
-Scotch Shoemaker-

During the late 1800s and early 1900s, the print media coverage of 'black issues' as reported in news publications like The Chicago Whip, Pittsburg Courier, and The Daily News revealed the way many post-reconstruction Freedmen and women viewed freedom as a force for improving their status or citizenship in the United States of America.

The African-American view of success in education, professions, government and society were parallel to many of the progressive ideals held by persons from other ethnic groups. Dating as far back as the 1800s throughout the early 1900s — whether members of Congress, inventors, real estate moguls, or millionaires — American success stories can be found within the African-American community[1].

Our patriarch's journey towards success started from Georgia into Alabama and was as dynamic as the ethnic status labeled on their US Federal Census forms for the mid to late 1800s.

While Cicero A. Kemp labeled himself "mulatto" on the 1880 US Federal Census, it was his first wife Anaca who was identified as "black" [2]. Some years later, having remarried in 1891 and residing in the rural mining town of Dora, Cicero A. Kemp and his new wife Aria Kemp (my maternal grandparents), as well as, their son James H. Kemp Sr. and a brother Louis Kemp were among the ranks of the town's miners and laborers.

Interestingly, between the 1800s to the 1920s, the labels for which members of the Kemp family designated their ethnic status or parent's birthplace on federal census forms would range from black, mulatto, negro, Alabama, Georgia, South Carolina and the "United States". Ultimately, according to the World

War I draft card of Cicero and Aria's only son -Joseph Rufus Kemp- he would declare that he was "African"[3].

Several astonishing facts about the Black Belt south during the late 1800s reveal key influences that may inspire the assumption of an "African" ethnicity by a southern "negro".

According to historical sources, the existence of an "African Town" near the ports south of Mobile, Alabama was the result of free West Africans aboard the last "illegal" Portuguese slave ship in 1860 – the Clotilda. Despite the abolishment of the international slave trade fifty-two years earlier, the ship was discovered trying to come under the cover of darkness. Fortunately, the well documented accounts of these survivors reveal that they were from the West African country of Benin, members from the Isha of the Yoruba people, and likely from the Bante region[4]. Therefore, historical precedent confirms that Cicero and Aria would raise children who were likely in contact with a specific African influence or awareness.

Life in these humble beginnings of Dora was like any other mining town - hard work for the parents and the children. The harsh reality of the town was documented in the US library of Congress' photo description caption of a group of Caucasian children of the 1800s. One of the children stated; "I've already met my 8 week requirement for education, so, now its time for work". If such was the life for the "white" Americans, then, one could imagine what life and education was like for the colored Americans with no schooling (or school for that matter).

Stemming from the slavery era until the present, the social dichotomy within African-American success stories is perhaps rooted in many of its communal expectations of survival. An ability to work inside and outside a local or national social system in order to achieve success as a doctor, lawyer or professional was an essential human characteristic and a basic survival necessity.[5]

The law of the land, at least in certain cities within America, justified a social order that limited or prohibited the educational, financial and social mobility of 'enslaved' African-Americans. Deterring economic self-sufficiency, the 1715 act in New York City made it forbidden for Blacks, Native-Americans, and mulattos (light-skinned blacks) from selling oysters in New York City. In South Carolina, some of the laws impacting many aspects of African American livelihood included requiring the wearing of 'negro cloth' of checkered or scotch plaids (1735), forbidding 'slaves' from raising live stock and forfeiting ownership of animals (1740), also, prohibited the teaching of mechanics or handicraft trades (1806).

The highest law of the land–the U.S. Constitution- considers slaves 3/5 of one white person, and, demands that fugitive slaves be returned to their masters (1790). Louisiana law orders African-American women to wear their hair in kerchief and forbids them to wear jewels and feathers (1823). Mississippi enacted laws making it prohibited to teach African-Americans how to read and write - the basic elements essential for learning (1823) [6].

Coupling many of these social realities with the atrocities of lynchings, denial of voting rights, and other essential social activities, many emancipated freedmen rushed at the federal government's announcement for opportunities to settle territorial lands like Oklahoma in 1889; thus, twenty-three years after the Emancipation Proclamation made the enslavement of African-Americans illegal throughout the United States, the quest among 'freed' African-Americans for a higher quality of intellectual attainment and social elevation was hastened.

An enterprising and industrious spirit for the establishment of self-governance, educational institutions, businesses and newspapers existed in laborers on the farm and oil fields. In the southwestern U.S. for example, the establishment of predominately African-American towns were being founded at such a rate that by 1930 there were twenty such towns in Oklahoma alone, comprising 7.2 percent of the state's population[7].

In the mist of this diverse consciousness there was a guiding theme among the Kemp family which rings true over one hundred sixty years later – believe in God, support the working man, organize for labor, women, and, unashamedly for their own community of African-Americans.

This theme was a principle of freedom that they were determined to maximize in order to build a world that they thought was best.

They would make the change that they believed needed to exist in America for them and their future generations.

The principle of freedom and fervor to express it was an ideal cultivated by their patriarchs, in their congregational church, Masonic lodges, and Odd Fellows organizations[8] – all of which was documented during their journeys through society as teachers, lawyers, policeman, etc.

The history of the Kemp's life can be traced through the legal documents of probate courts, federal census, college records, marriage licenses, directories, draft cards, birth or death records and more.

The belief system and pioneering spirit of freedom fueled their drive to make change for themselves and future generations.

Following the civil war at the turn of the twentieth century and the subsequent emancipation proclamation, Cicero and Aria were focusing on sending their children to school even though there were no local elementary or high schools for colored or "freedmen" – a fact of life that was clearly evident in rural mining towns like Dora, Alabama[9]. However, it wasn't until January of 1888--twenty-five years after the Emancipation Proclamation—that the Slater Normal School for Colored Children was created in nearby

Birmingham[8]. Subsequently, the Kemp's invested in education for their son James H. Kemp, Sr. [10], boarding schools for their daughter Julia, and teacher training for Marjorie at Talladega College in Alabama[11].

Since there were no free schools in the state of Alabama, the families of high school students had to pay a monthly fee of one dollar and fifty cents[12].

Following Cicero's death in 1911, the records from the four year probate court proceedings had an accounting of payment for "boarding school fees for Julia", as well as, fees for the Masonic Lodges and Odd Fellows orders[13].

The benefits of educating their oldest daughter Marjorie were immediately noticeable from her correspondence and signatures on the administration paperwork of the 1916 probate proceedings for her uncle Louis Kemp.

Following the death of uncle Louis, their son- Joseph Rufus Kemp- would become the administrator of the estate by Angeline's (Marjorie) concession[14]; also, according to the Birmingham directory listings of 1916 and 1918, Marjorie was teaching at the newly built Slater Normal School for Colored Children[15].

A prominent Slater School educator—Arthur Parker—noted in his biography that during the late 1800s and early 1900s the leaders of logic for the African-American community were the preachers and teachers; moreover, the teachers understood their mission at Slater Normal school to be preparing the next wave of future teachers and leaders for colored people[16].

Furthermore, Parker noted, it was from the local Congregational Church in Birmingham that the children of the prominent colored professionals (who comprised the majority of the church's membership) greatly increased the size of enrollment of the Slater Normal School[17].

Since preparing teachers and preachers was the focus of many universities with Normal Departments like Talladega College in Alabama, then, Cicero and Aria Kemp's investment in their children's education would foster the transformative force of freedom.

(photo below) World War I Draft Card of great uncle Joseph Rufus Kemp. Place of birth is Dora, Alabama. Born on November 29, 1894. [photo from: United States, Selective Service System. *World War I Selective Service System Draft Registration Cards, 1917-1918.*

(Left Photo) Sadie Lee Kemp holding baby James Kemp, Jr,

(Middle Photo) Joseph Rufus Kemp – "the African"

(Left) Arleene & Celestine Kemp-Jefferies

Love At Our Roots   James H. Commander

CHAPTER 2

A MIRACLE OF THE GOOD SHEPHERD
1922 - 1944

*"Pray for powers equal to your tasks.
Then the doing of your work shall be no miracle,
But you shall be a miracle."*
                                        -Phillips Brooks-

Excitement about new possibilities for using freedom to inspire change was clearly on the minds of my great grandmother Aria Thompson Kemp. The influenza outbreak had hit Alabama cities like Birmingham so hard that the Industrial High school for coloreds was converted into a hospital for coloreds[1].

By comparing her replies for where her parents were born on the U.S. Federal Census — Alabama in 1910 and the United States in 1920 — she was establishing new social directions for her children[2]; moreover, following the death of both uncle Louis E. Kemp and the family's patriarch Cicero Adams Kemp, Aria traveled with four of her daughters and one son to Chicago while the other uncle — James Horace Kemp, Sr. — settled in Oklahoma with his wife Sadie Lee.

The Kemp family in Oklahoma provided safe houses for officials of the National Association for the

Advancement of Colored People (NAACP). James H. Kemp Sr. would travel from the western frontier into the mid western state of Indiana while active in civil rights group and taking his son James H. Kemp, Jr. with him to the NAACP meetings[3].

By tracing the life of my grandmother Marjorie Angeline Kemp from Dora, Alabama to Chicago, one could see how the force of freedom was used to change their life's direction. A "second Negro renaissance" was emerging in cities like New York and Chicago, thus, there was a lot of excitement among the social and educational circles or the black communities. According to Francis Taylor who was the roommate and future sister-in-law to the legendary dancer Katherine Dunham, the popular chant at the time was "Negritude! Negritude is beautiful!".

During her five years as a postal clerk, she and

her sisters were engaged in civic activities, education, and the establishment of a church that would later be known as the Good Shepherd Congregational Church. Upon arriving in Chicago in 1918, Marjorie's experience working at the social service department of the US Steel Company in Pittsburgh, Pennsylvania, and becoming a member of the National Federation of Post Office Clerks, Local No. 1 were indications of her early commitment to organizing labor, women, and African-Americans.

The period of 1922 and 1923 was a rather busy year for the Kemp sisters. Marjorie was awarded a six-month scholarship to the National Women's Trade Union League's training school. Many of the training school classes were taught at the University of Chicago were she had already taken up work.

During the period when it operated under the

name of the Langley Avenue Congregational Church from 1922 through 1924, her sister -Juanita Kemp- was active as one of the original members of Good Shepherd.

Juanita was a Sunday school teacher while the church was in the Henderson's home on 4821 Langley Avenue, as well as, the secretary when it moved and changed its name to the Michigan Avenue Congregational Church in the year of 1926.

While maintaining an active religious life, Juanita Kemp would enroll in the education department of the Chicago Normal College in 1926.

Although unmarried to Marjorie at the time, my future grandfather – Henry A. Spaulding - was also enrolled in Chicago Normal College. [He would eventually be listed as a "lodger" on the 1940 U.S. Federal Census for the Kemp's address located in the southwest sector of the Hyde Park township – 4821 S. Vincennes.]

During the year of 1929, indications of the Kemp family's active social, educational, and religious life would become evident as well as prominent. A fulfillment of their parents' investment in education, Juanita Kemp graduated from the Chicago Normal School in 1929 and would be assigned a teaching position in the Chicago Public Schools.

Another indication of their forward mobility was discovered in a one hundred year old family heirloom (a handmade historical scrapbook made by Marjorie Kemp and entrusted to me by my Aunt Juanita Kemp).

The scrapbook contained several handbills from the January 1929 launch of America's first integrated theatre — The Cube at the University of Chicago.

The playbill contained a who's who listing of

actors, actresses, professors, and patrons. Activist Ida B. Wells, Mr. and Mrs. Dr. George C. Hall (confidant of Booker T. Washington), also, Chicago Defender founders Mr. and Mrs. Robert Abott were among a few of the notable patrons. Moreover, the bill included the first ever stage appearance of Catherine Dunham as "Sally" in Paul Green's play The Man Who Died at Twelve O'Clock; as well as, a new award winning play Dreamy Kid by Eugene O'neil featuring Frances Taylor, Brunetta Mosely Lewis of the pioneering Alpha Kappa Alpha sorority of Chicago, and Brunetta Barnett (whose name also appeared in the 1929 Good Shepherd Congregational Church member directory).

The fervor of racial progress was not only clear in the worlds of performing arts and academia — Negro pride in Chicago was also evident among the professional class of blacks from the Kemp's church.

Already growing by leaps and bounds, the church, by November of 1928, had moved to 5700 S. Prairie Avenue and changed the name to the Church of the Good Shepherd, Congregational. The increase in activities were a far cry from holding services with several members in the Henderson's home from 1922 to 1924; with 24 charter members in 1925; and 55 members in 1927. The church demonstrated its growth to 605 members at a 1,000% increase during 22 months. Supporting the church's report of a financial increase of $80 per month in 1928 to $1,000 per month in 1929; also, Sunday attendance of 38 in 1927 to 1,000 attendees by 1929, the members were published in a 1929 directory.

However, while touting the credentials of newly appointed Rev. Harold M. Kinsley as possessing a B.A. from Talladega College, 1908; and a B.D. from Yale University in 1911, a larger social project was on the horizon.

The social project was destined to launch the church into the forefront of the exodus of Negroes from southern states burdened by Jim Crow laws into the evolving mid-western "promise land" of Chicago. There should not have been a surprise about the ambitions of a minister who was a "special investigator of Negro Exadus", as well as, his having served in several capacities of "Negro committees" or "Negro work". Rev. Kingsley and his legion of church members were about to embark on a huge social service undertaking – the establishment of the Good Shepherd Community Center.

While my grandmother Marjorie was entering her second year of teacher training at the Normal Department in Talladega College, by 1908 Kingsley had recently completed his B.A. in Theological training at

Talladega and was starting his first year at Yale; Moreover, he had an equally significant social indoctrination on race relations while attending a college based in a state that was a hotbed of activity during the American Civil War and Creek Indian War.

Since its inception, his alma mater's founders (the American Missionary Association) intended to empower the recently freed from slavery with the aptitude for "self-governance". According to the AMA's manual for Talladega College in 1900, a formula for success was for the Negro students to "work out your own salvation" [7].

The AMA would build a church as a supplement to the hundreds of schools they were building for the education of the freedmen. Therefore, Kingsley's direct mission was to participate and lead the type of social change that would facilitate the transitioning of post-slavery blacks suffering from underdevelopment into the mainstream of America's best citizens.

The Episcopalian or Congregational churches were the religious institutions favored by socially mobile blacks due to the formal and culturally refined environments. A well educated clergy, small membership and a reputation for giving financial support towards establishing black colleges during the late 1800s was the appeal of the Congregational church. Lawrence Otis Graham notes that the Church of the Good Shepherd in Chicago dominated the religious scene for 'upper-class' blacks during the early 1900s[8].

A cultural distinction between African-Americans from the south in comparison to northern blacks could be seen in the motives for choosing a church home and a college to attend. For example, during the post-emancipation to progressive years, the members of the economically and politically (aka- 'black elites') would attend black colleges associated with the American Missionary Association (AMA) like Howard University in Washington, or, attend traditional ivy-league schools like Harvard, Yale or the University of Chicago.

Collegiate and Christian links between the Rev. Kingsley and members of the Kemp family were in existence two decades prior to any committee meetings for determining a new pastor of the Church of the Good Shepherd in 1927. As a matter of fact, a congregational church connection with the Kemp family was maintained while Marjorie Angeline Kemp was teaching at the Slater Normal School for Colored Children from 1916-1918.

The children of the professional members from the First Congregational Church of Birmingham were the main factors for the increase of student enrollment from 95 to 325 students in one month, as well as, the school's expansion from rooms of the church into a new school building[4]; Therefore, this common fusion of social and spiritual enthusiasm fueled their personal and community fervor for utilizing freedom to build a better reality for the African-American Congregational Church community of Dora and Birmingham, Alabama.

    Serving as a teacher with the Chicago Public Schools, church steward, and community organizer, my grandmother Marjorie was fulfilling her role as the bearer of the family's torchlight. Her pioneering work as an educator for coloreds in Alabama was long recognized by W.E. B. Dubois in The Crisis magazine-- she had maintained that relationship through regular correspondence with Dubois for his local speaking engagements, fee collections, and even the writing of his novel Dark Princess in 1927.

Applying the Kemp family philosophy of progressive social mobility would contribute to her ascension as the president of the Illinois Democratic Woman's Charity and Employment League in 1931.

She celebrated the accomplishment with the iconic sociologist and activist W.E.B. Dubois as he wrote about "understanding now why Mr. Cermack won" [the mayoral election of Chicago].
She reminded him that it was he who earlier said: "Cermack will win if Marjorie gives him her ok".

Clearly, the proof that constitutional freedoms legally acknowledged following the civil war was to be fully exercised for the benefit of the church, family, and community.

While Kingsley and the members of Good

Shepherd were evolving as a church, over the next few years they were also busy in the church's basement.

Housed in the basement of Good Shepherd from 1936 to1939, Horace Cayton and the center's board of directors, the US Government's Worker's Progress Administration program (WPA), and the Chicago Board of Education were focused on creating a community outreach institution –The Good Shepherd Community Center.

An announcement for starting new programs, and the construction of buildings near the church was made in December 1939. Appointing Horace Cayton with an eighteen-thousand dollar salary as the center's director, the Church of the Good Shepherd would embark on creating "the largest African-American settlement house in the world" [18].

(Right Photo) The 1929 Certificate of Graduation from the Chicago Normal College for Juanita Kemp.

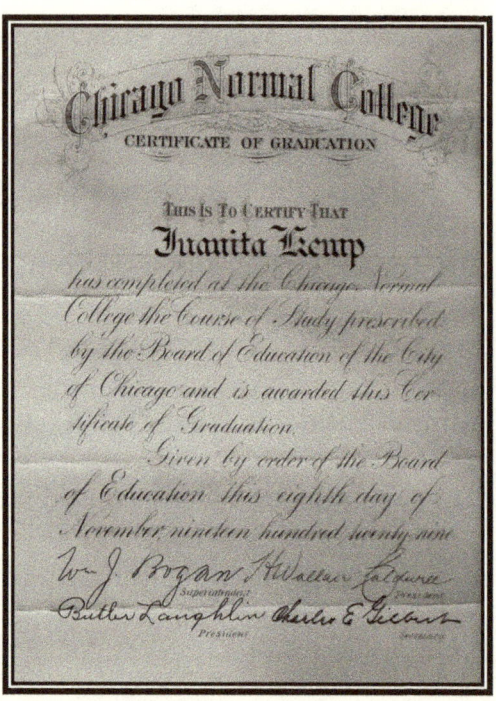

(Bottom photo) Grandpa Henry Allen Spaulding in the 1926 student yearbook for the Chicago Normal College. He would graduate and later obtain a law degree.

PATRONS

Miss Polly Ames
Mr. and Mrs. Robert Abbott
Mr. Elf Anderson
Miss Zonia Baber

Mr. and Mrs. Balduf
Mrs. Ida B. W. Barnett
Mr. and Mrs. Jesse Binga
Mr. and Mrs. Adolf Bolm

Dr. and Mrs. M. O. Bousfield
Dr. Fay-Cooper Cole
Mr. Albert Dunham
Dr. Ellsworth Feris

Judge and Mrs. Albert George
Miss Irene Gaines
Mrs. Wendell Green
Mr. and Mrs. G. C. Hall

Mr. Robert Harshe

Mrs. Lulu Lawson
Mr. and Mrs. Cary B. Lewis
Mr. and Mrs. E. W. Lunquist
Miss Helen F. Mackenzie

Mr. Dexter Masters
Mr. and Mrs. Nelson
Mr. Sterling North
Mr. Anthony Overton

Mr. and Mrs. Rothschild
Mr. and Mrs. Edward Sapir
Mr. and Mrs. T. W. Stevens
Mr. and Mrs. Lorado Taft

Dr. and Mrs. Chas. Thompson
Miss Laura van Pappelendam
Mr. Dudley Crafts Watson
Mr. Albert Widdefield

(Photo) Patron listing for Cube Theater debut with icons like Ida b. Wells, Robert Abbott, Dr, George C. Hall, Judge Albert George, Jesse Binga, and many more scholars, and professions.

(Photo) Debut of the "An Art Exhibition by Negro Artist of Chicago" at The Cube theater launch in January of 1929. The artist -William Eduard Scott, Arthur Diggs, William Farrow, Charles Dawson, Richard Barte, and K.D. Ganaway.

```
                    THE CUBE
              1538 East 57th Street
                    CHICAGO

                    Presents

        AN ART EXHIBITION By NEGRO ARTISTS OF CHICAGO
                   -----+-----

RICHMOND BARTE                K. D. GANAWAY

1. Head Of A Boy              14. The Arms Of Construction
2. The Tortured Negro         15. Me
3. "Garbage"                  16. Thru Chicago
4. A Study                    17. In Tow On Chicago River
5. Head Of The Tortured Negro 18. The Old Museum
6. Head Of A Negro            19. The Garner's Cart
7. Bust Of "_____"         20. House Wife
8. Donald Jeffrey Hayes       21. Indiana Sand Dunes
                              22. The Spirit Of Transportation
ARTHUR DIGGS                  23. Near Wilson Indiana

9. Landscape                  WM. EDOUARD SCOTT

CHARLES DAWSON                24. Negro Head
                              25. Wrigley Reflections
10. Searchlights

WILLIAM M. FARROW             COMMITTEE OF ADMISSION

11. Aida                      C. J. BULLIET
12. Dream Time                WILLIAM SCHWARTZ
13. The Ringling Home         EDWARD ROTHSCHILD
```

(Photo) The Church of the Good Shepherd Congregational Directory and Manual cover of 1929. A listing of thousands of members names, financial reports, and addresses along with business advertisements.

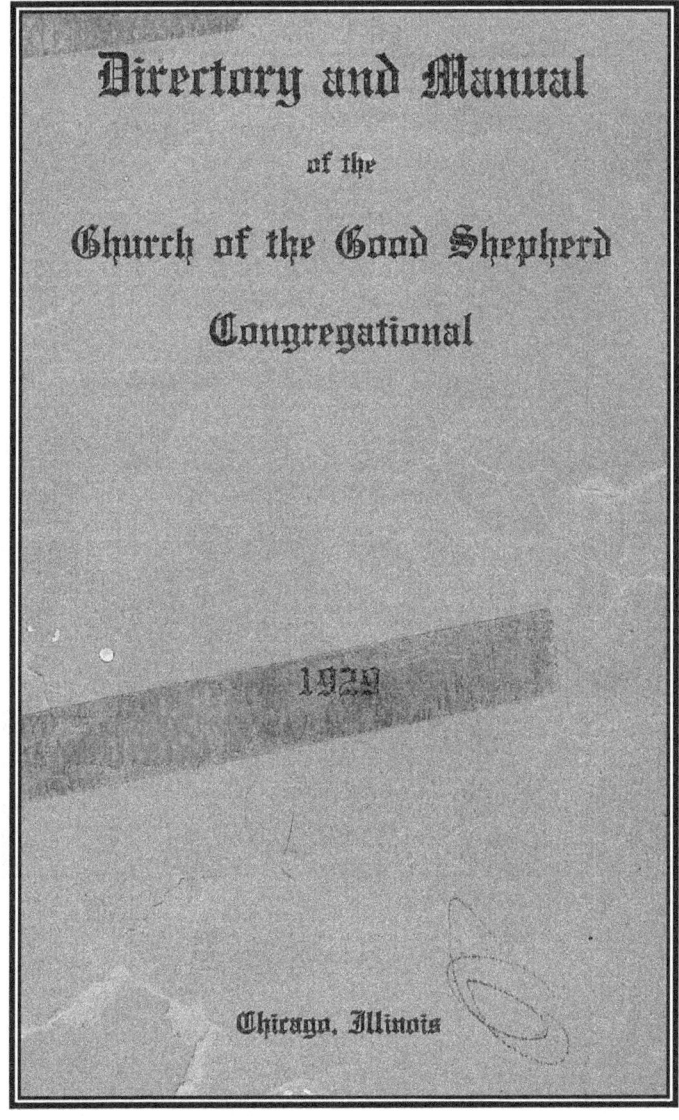

THE BANK OF THE COMMUNITY

In the current developments of the Mid-South Side our facilities are unexcelled.

BINGA STATE BANK
STATE AT 35th STREET

35TH STREET ARCADE BUILDING
N. W. Corner State and 35th Streets

The Auditorium with a seating capacity of 700, is the most beautiful and magnificent hall in the city. Especially adapted to parties, receptions and community meetings. Rate upon appliction.

PHONE CALUMET 6302

(Photo) Binga was inspired to establish his own bank in 1908, he put a full-page advertisement in the Good Shepherd directory and manual.

Harold M. Kingsley in the 1929 Good Shepherd Directory. He was a graduate of Talladega College in Alabama a 1908 graduate and current student at Yale Divinity School.

(Right photo) Cover of W.E. DuBois' book Dark Princess.

(Bottom photo) The October 10, 1927 letter from W.E. DuBois to Grandmother Marjorie Kemp for her support with research data for his upcoming book Dark Princess.

```
                October 10, 1927.

Miss Marjorie Kemp,
4821 Vincennes Avenue,
Chicago, Illinois.

My dear Marjorie:

        I want your help if you can
spare the time.

        I have written a novel which
Harcourt, Brace and Company are
going to publish in the early
spring. A part of the scene I have
laid in Chicago. I want some definite
information about things which
I know only in a general way. Do
you think you can get this informa-
tion for me and send it sometime
this month? If it is too much
trouble, never mind. But if you
can do it I shall appreciate it.

                Very sincerely yours,

WEBD/DN
Enclosure
```

(Photo) The letter from Grandmother Marjorie Kemp to W.E.B. DuBois announcing her presidential victory of the Illinois Democratic Woman's Charity and Employment League of 1931.

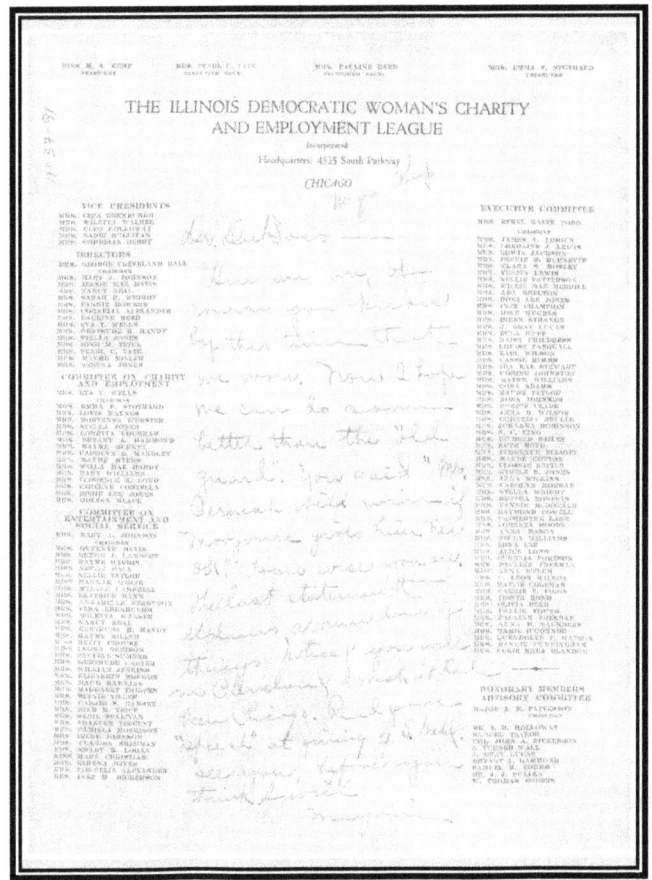

(Photo) A War Ration booklet for Aria Kemp in the 1940s.

4

150895 BL

UNITED STATES OF AMERICA
OFFICE OF PRICE ADMINISTRATION

WAR RATION BOOK FOUR

Issued to A r i a   K e m p
(Print first, middle, and last names)

Complete address 4821   Vincennes

Chicago   Ill.

READ BEFORE SIGNING

In accepting this book, I recognize that it remains the property of the United States Government. I will use it only in the manner and for the purposes authorized by the Office of Price Administration.

Void if Altered
(Signature)

It is a criminal offense to violate rationing regulations.

OPA Form R-145   16—35570-1

(photo) WPA data from the study of the Negro by Horace Clayton, Jr. in the basement of the Good Shepherd Congregational Church community center, Chicago, Illinois, April 1940 Photographer unidentified.

Love At Our Roots   James H. Commander

CHAPTER 3

STAGGERD NOT AT THE PROMISE
1950 - 1975

"I endure all things for the sake of God's own people;
so that they also may obtain salvation...
and with it eternal glory."
-2 Timothy 2:10
BIBLE [KJV]

Gaining momentum following emancipation, industrialization, and migrations, the force for freedom became a vital tool for creating new family standards. One transformation of ideals could be seen, shortly after the family moved onto Bowen Avenue on Chicago's Southeast side, during a response to the "nativity" question on the 1920 U.S. Census. Our great-grandmother Aria Kemp, following my grandmother Marjorie's arrival to Chicago in 1918, had changed her previous answer for ethnicity from a singular state (like Georgia or Alabama) to the "United States"[1].

This change in social identity was a clear indication of having recognized the social impact and benefits from the new freedoms of post-slavery, as well as, post World War I.

Much of the family's zeal and commitment for upward mobility became prevalent by the 1940s into the new decade. The sweat equity from work, academic development, and religious commitment were starting to foster the mustard seeds of faith in freedom as the third generation of Kemps began seizing the reins of the family traditions.

Specifically, community and social traditions were growing rapidly as the Good Shepherd Community Center became a major influence in the Chicago Renaissance with support from the leading scholars, professionals, labor leaders, artists and more[2]. For example, Langston Hughes had moved into the center in order to establish a theater house and performance troupe – The Skyloft Players in 1939-1940 (although he left after debuting his play "Sun Do Move)[3]. The "father of the blues"-W.C. Handy, members of the Katherine Dunham Dance Group, and novelist Richard Wright were other notables from the creative professions who participated in activities of the Good Shepherd Community Center[4] (which was named the Parkway Community House by 1942). Also, speakers at the Parkway House included labor leaders like A. Phillip Randolph of the BSCP and James H. Kemp Jr. who had been elected president of the Builders Employees International Union, local 189 of the AFL[5].

During the mid 1940s, our future aunt Maida Springer-Kemp was emerging as a labor leader who was recognized and awarded by Mary McCloud Bethune as one of the outstanding Negro women[6] in 1945. A licensed beautician, who was a student at Annie T. Malone's School of Beauty and Culture, she opted to become a secretary at the Poro and Malone Schools instead of working as a hair stylist like her mother. Since her time as a young boarding school student in New Jersey, some of the greatest intellectual minds like W.E. B. Dubois, Paul Robeson, Judge William Hasting, and Lester Granger were the school speakers or teachers who shaped her expectations of accomplishment[7]; Moreover, her sense of self-worth and cultural pride was instilled by her

Panamanian mother—Adina Forrest Stewart (Carrington)—who was a loyal member of the Universal Negro Improvement Association (UNIA), held stock in the Terry Holding Association (a self-help agency affiliated with the Marcus Garvey Movement), and a nurse within the Black Cross.[8] Thus, Aunt Maida was immersed in and keenly aware of the cultural continuum extending from her mother and father—Harold Stewart, a West Indian emigrant to Panama following his education in England[9].

During her transition into adulthood, Maida became employed in the labor work of the garment industry and became active in the labor unions. Her personal growth moved through various stages en route to joining the union [12]. Possessing pride for being a U.S. citizen, she would remain passionate about her efforts on behalf of working men and women despite having to endure government officials, as she describes, "talking to us as though we were scum"[13].

Her years of labor work and training would prompt an offer to her for the vice-presidency in the International Ladies Garment Worker's Union (ILGWU), however, it was without a union membership base, so, she chose to become a trouble shooter throughout North and South Carolina, Georgia and Florida in 1965. Her acceptance of the Midwest directorship of the A. Phillip Randolph Institute by 1969, allowed her to give attention to the Chicago land area before traveling to Africa to work on behalf of the unions, women workers, and African-Americans—an endeavor that lead to her and uncle James H. Kemp jointly receiving the Walter Phillip Reuthers Humanitarian Award in 1971[14].

Our Aunt Maida would eventually return to Africa in 1973 and become a staff member with the union, as well as, provide consultation to an AFL-CIO affiliate[15]— the African-American Labor Center (AALC).

The life patterns of the aforementioned members of the Kemp family reveal some similarities in academic, social, and religious preparations as taken by Maida Kemp. Her personal development went from the "Garvey movement, the American Church, the black cultural experience in a school, to the labor movement"[16]. Whether driven by abolitionist, social reformers, or labor unions, answering the meaningful call for individual and communal betterment became a specific example to live by, as well as, instill into future generations an enduring family tradition[17].

(Far Left Photo)
Maida Springer-Kemp while working with the Int'l Ladies Garment Worker's Union (ILGWU).

(Right Photo)
Uncle James H. Kemp in 1937. Labor Leader, Athlete, Member of Omega Psi Pi, and Graduate of John Marshall Law school.

(Mid Photo)
Mary M. Bethune and Maida Springer-Kemp in 1945.

(Bottom Photo)
James H. Kemp, Maida Springer-Kemp at U.N. with Holy See in 1963.

(Left Photo) James H. Kemp, Maida Springer-Kemp, A. Philip Randolph in 1965.

(Bottom Photo) James and Maida Kemp get Reuter's Humanitarian Award 1971.

CHAPTER 4

ENDURE ALL THINGS
1950 - 1975

"I endure all things for the sake of God's own people;
so that they also may obtain salvation...
and with it eternal glory."
-2 Timothy 2:10
BIBLE [KJV]

By the 1940s and 1950s, the Kemp family had purchased their own apartment building at 4871 S. Vincennes[9], most of the Kemp sisters were certified teachers in the Chicago Board of Education system, James H. Kemp and Marjorie Kemp were labor leaders, and the family's church had become an institutional cornerstone of the African-American migration from their parents' southern home states (like Georgia, Alabama, and South Carolina) into the northern metropolis of Chicago[10].

The maintenance of these social activities and personal growth was to continue into the emergence of a third generational Kemp family in the 1950s. My mother, Pamela Sydney Spaulding-Commander, was born in 1946, and with her sister—Patricia Spaulding-Muhammad—was raised by newlyweds Marjorie Kemp and Henry A. Spaulding[11] (married October 1940 in Jackson County, Iowa City). Although the two siblings would share a similar childhood in the rural area of Cassopolis, Michigan, as well as, the more urbanized Hyde Park community, their adult lives would go in separate directions.

Pamela was fascinated by ballet dancing and would often be captured in childhood photographs wearing her ballet shoes. Her academic training at the University of Chicago's Lab School in the 1960's (or U-High as it is referred to by faculty and students), also, her graduation from High Park High School on the South Side of Chicago in 1964, lead to her receiving a scholarship to a historical Black college; However, Pamela, following her creative passions, would chose to pursue a modeling career at a school located in downtown Chicago. Despite marrying several times and giving birth to eight children, she would suffer (early in her young adult life) from a series of nervous breakdowns, a case of schizophrenia, and dementia in her elder years.

The elder sister, Patricia was also trained in the

fine arts and used her literary skills to write for the teen section of the Defender newspaper. She would be introduced to her future husband during a meeting at their Hyde Park home while her father was discussing the selling of some of the family's nearby property as a means of providing more security for their neighbor –the Most Honorable Elijah Muhammad. She would later marry the neighbor's son--Herbert (Jabir) Muhammad--who was the representative for the business affairs of the Nation of Islam, as well as, the manager of the heavyweight champion Muhammad Ali. Ultimately, she would graduate from college with post doctorate degrees for specialized nursing and receive accolades for her service to the medical community, as well as Mayor Daley for her achievements. She has two daughters, grandchildren, and great grand children.

Being well established as pillars in the political and professional spheres of the Chicago community by the 1960s (the African-American society, specifically), the shadow of the third generation of Kemp family members was cast far and wide for future progeny. For example, the Kemp sisters had retired from successful careers with the Chicago Board of Education; Marjorie Kemp-Spaulding was serving as co-chair of benefits for the Randall House school for inter-racial boys[12]; James H. Kemp, Jr. had become the president re-elect of the Builders Union[13], also board member of the N.A.A.C.P.[14], Illinois Fair Employment Practices Commission[15] (selected by Governor Otto Kerner) in 1962, a delegate for the revision of the Illinois State Constitution in 1969, and board member to the newly formed Rapid Transit Authority[16] (RTA) in 1974. Yet, social advancement wasn't the only areas where the Kemp family had improvement.

By the 1970s, the Kemp family had upheld a tradition in which many African-Americans from the post-emancipation proclamation era firmly believed—land is the basis of independence. The acquisition of real estate properties throughout Chicago's Hyde Park township, as well as, land in the rural town Cassopolis, Michigan (a former hub for affluent African-Americans) was another principle of freedom exemplified one hundred years up from slavery.

It is not surprising that fertile lands for raising a variety of crops like corn and alfalfa were sought after by the Honorable Elijah Muhammad in 1971. Responding to his inquiry about acquiring some land, my grandmother Marjorie Kemp informed him that over 60 acres of farmland could be made available for rent. Also, in later years, my great aunt Juanita Kemp would lend her support to the upkeep of the private DeLena Day School located on Hyde Park Boulevard, thus, staying true to Booker T. Washington, W.E.B. DuBois, and the American Missionary Association's vision of fostering the freedmen's ability to educate and teach themselves.

DeLena was founded by Louis and Lena House[17], but operated by their children—fellow congregational church adherents and former Alabama natives Bishop William Moore and his wife Mrs. Desmond Moore[18] (thus the school's first letters "De" and the last four letters "Lena"). Shortly after the passing of his wife[19], Bishop Moore sold the school to Mrs. Crocket in the early 1970s[20]. Following Juanita Kemp's retirement from the Chicago Public Schools, she would join the teaching staff and provide funding in order to keep the school operational. Well into the closing of DeLena Day School in the late 1980s[21], Juanita would uphold the Kemp family's tradition of using the force of freedom in preparing the future leaders through teaching or building private schools.

A particularly honorable achievement for the family was the 1970 election of James H. Kemp, Jr. to the board of trustees of Talladega College in Alabama[22] –the same school where his Aunt Angeline [Marjorie A. Kemp] attended for Normal College[23] in1908; Moreover, this was the collegiate institution where the pastor of the Good Shepherd Congregational Church—Rev. Arthur Grey—became the first Black president[24] in 1952, thus, symbolically and cultural on behalf of the broader African-American community, completing an exemplary journey of one hundred years from the Kemp family's humble beginnings as pre-emancipated "farm laborers"[25] and post-emancipated coal miners of Walker County, Alabama[26].

Since their acceptance of the mantle of freedom and its accompanying responsibility after legalized slavery in the black belt south, the Kemp family had fervently pressed forward seeking change for themselves and their communities. The twenty-five years of progress from the 1950s into the mid 1970s was a demonstration of the family's resolve to dispel any myth about the capacity of African-Americans to evolve from being "mere laborers" into leaders and standard bearers of the African-American citizenry, as well as, productive citizens of America.

Since a good race with the baton of freedom had been ran for three generations, then, the ever-watchful elders had an interest in handing over the torchlight of the family's traditions; However, carrying the weight of such a legacy would demand that adequate preparation be made by whomever would shoulder such a duty.

(Left Photo) Pamela Commander in "ballet shoes" at 1957 Easter Tea of the Good Shepherd Church. (Bottom photos) Pamela Commander in Hyde Park H.S. graduation. Pamela Commander in the 1960 Yearbook of The University of Chicago Lab School or "U-high".

(Right Photo) James Kemp speaks as AFL Leader at the Parkway or Good Shepherd Community Center.

NAPE Installation At Parkway, Jan. 6

The Chicago branch of the National Alliance of Postal Employees will install officers Sunday, Jan. 6, at 4 P. M., at the Parkway Community Center, 5120 South Parkway. The oath of office will be administered by the outstanding member of the branch, the able national president, Ashby B. Carter.

Newly elected officers who will serve for the next two years are Leon J. Hillman, president; Smalley Cook, vice president; Robert Birdsong, corresponding recording secretary; James J. S. Keys, financial secretary; Vernon A. Cannon, assistant financial secretary; Walter Walker, treasurer; Ashby G. Smith, editor of Voice; Whitney Ewell, trustee. Board members are German S. White, U. V. Reynolds, Jackson Taylor, Alfred Simpson, Raymr, Morris Herron, wford and Otis M.

UPON THE RECOMMENDATION OF THE FACULTY
AND BY AUTHORITY OF THE BOARD OF GOVERNORS OF
STATE COLLEGES AND UNIVERSITIES

ILLINOIS TEACHERS COLLEGE: CHICAGO SOUTH

HAS CONFERRED UPON

JUANITA KEMP

THE DEGREE OF

MASTER OF SCIENCE IN EDUCAT

WITH ALL OF THE RIGHTS, HONORS AND PRIVILEGES BE
THAT DEGREE. IN WITNESS THEREOF THIS DIPLOMA
THIS TWENTY-SECOND DAY OF APRIL, 1966.

REMARKS
BY

JAMES H. KEMP
President

BUILDING SERVICE
JOINT COUNCIL No. 1 OF CHICAGO

TUESDAY, FEBRUARY 1, 1966

(Top Photo) The Master Degree of Juanita Kemp from Teacher's College in Chicago.

(Right Photo) James H. Kemp re-election speech for presidency of Building Service Joint Council No. 1 of Chicago. (

(Photo) James H. Kemp is elected as a trustee of the Talladega College in Alabama.

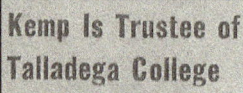

Kemp Is Trustee of Talladega College

James H. Kemp has been named a member of the board of trustees of Talladega College, sponsored by the American Missionary Mission in Talladega, Ala.

Kemp is a member of the Executive Board of the Chicago Federation of Labor and Industrial Union Council and president of Service Employees Local 189. He is a member of the Illinois Fair Employment Practices Commission and is active in civic and political organizations in the community.

Talladega was founded in 1867 as a primary school. While dedicated to basic fundamentals of the Christian faith, it is non-sectarian and interracial in both faculty and student body.

JAMES H. KEMP

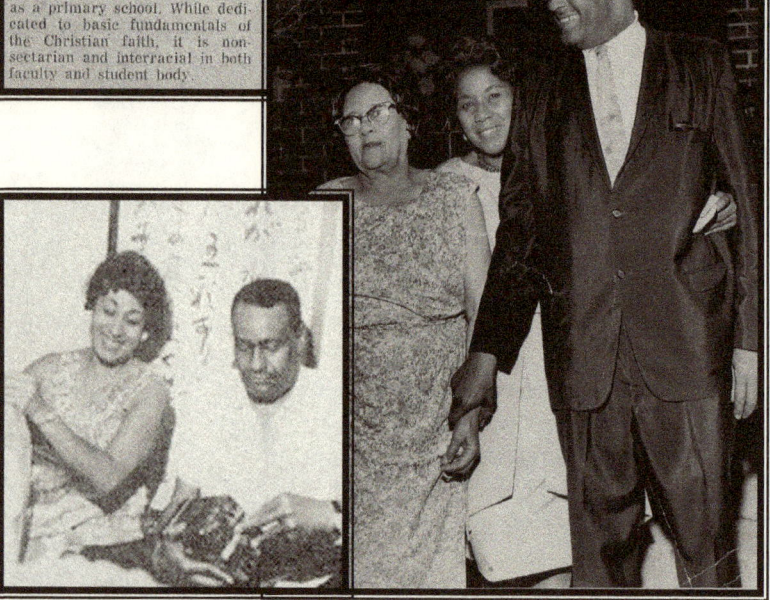

(Bottom Left Photo) James Kemp and fiancé Betty Everett, an Urban League organizer who died in a tragic car crash in 1963. (Bottom Right Photo) James H. Kemp, Maida Springer-Kemp, and Aunt Kemp 1960s.

(Left Photo) A hand written letter for a land offer from Marjorie Kemp to Elijah Muhammad in the 1970s. (Right photo) A type written version of the above letter in the 1970s.

(Left Photo) A letter offering land that was producing alfalfa, and other crops, from Marjorie Kemp to Elijah Muhammad in the 1970s.

Love At Our Roots   James H. Commander

CHAPTER 5

TO WHOM MUCH IS GIVEN

1975 - FUTURE

"You are stronger than you think!"
-Momma Pam-

If I have the gift of prophecy and can fathom all mysteries and all knowledge, and if I have a faith that can move mountains, but do not have love, I am nothing. Love is patient, love is kind.
1 Corinthians 13:2 and 13:4 [NIV]

"You've got the world in your hands – so don't drop it!"
-Aunt Patricia Spaulding-Muhammad-

Despite the very humble beginnings, one thing was made crystal clear during the early years of my youth – momma loved me.

My earliest and fondest memories of momma Pam ranges from her tender counsel about integrity (criticisms or character), the comforts of nature (botany or the lakefront), her love for the fine arts (poetry, jazz and dance), her appreciation for education (museums and universities), and her love for her children, many of her elders, and the favorite uncle whom she named me after – James H. Kemp, Jr.

Predominantly, my mother's kindness and encouragement for me to excel during the developmental years of my childhood were reflections of her upbringing and family influences. Whether it was cultural refinement or self-preservation, my mother made the time to instill some of the critical elements of our family traditions for my social, spiritual and educational foundations.

Since my birth occurred on May 25, 1971, many of the Kemp family's great social achievements had already occurred, however, some of the best were yet to come.

During the developmental years of my youth, the Parkways community between sixty-seventh and Stoney Island on the east and west to Jeffery was the area where my mother lived. While we were bouncing from one dilapidated building to the next (usually following a building condemnation), our pride was bolstered by several sources including my mother, the local elementary school, Cynthia McKinney's community center, and some in-laws of the Edwards and Blackmans.

Maneuvering the volatile social waters of the local neighborhood was possible due to a set of unique survival skills that became critical later in my life.

Some of my mother's most memorable survival lessons included feeding a zeal for learning, giving mutual respect to people, self-defense, and keeping my head up regardless of who or what is being said or done to me (i.e. confidence and pride in my unique self).

She demonstrated these lessons to me by encouraging me to pursue academics which led to my reading and math test scores being two grades ahead of the fourth grade level at Parkside Elementary; instructing me to pick up the nearest weapon to protect myself from personal harm; and, sharply discerning whether a person was going to buy me clothes rather than critique my appearance. It was through these instances that she instilled in me some sense of integrity.

Although her strong sense of pride would prevent receiving too much help from concerned school teachers or neighbors, she made sure to nurture a sense of inner dignity by reminding me of my "rich blood or tastes"—a fact about her own childhood that would be revealed to me later in my teenage years.

Several teachers at Parkside fostered my self-pride for excellence instead of self-pity. An exemplary cultivator of my character during adolescence was the beloved gym teacher—Mr. Drummond (RIP)—who offered to buy my gym shoes in order to play on the school's basketball team; Also, in third grade—Mrs. Jackson—who donated several boxes of clothes to me. A neighborhood peer—Pete Robinson (RIP)—was a defender of my personal pride on at least three occasions in grammar, high school, and adult hood.

Although the community was full of protectors and predators, my blessing was to have been mostly surrounded by people possessing an attitude for being community guardians. Ms. Cynthia, for instance, as the director of the local community center located on the same block where we once lived, was one of those local protectors. The recreational activities of bus trips to skating rinks, amusement parks, cook outs, or arts and crafts in the center were places of refuge—especially since the southern boarder of our community was on the battle front lines for the super-gang rivalry between members of the Black Gangster Disciples and the El-Rukns (or Blackstone Rangers).

Interestingly, my band of friends from the neighborhood shunned the destructive lifestyle of gangbangers and embraced a constructive work ethic, as well as, the performance and creative arts. The local community center, peers in the neighborhood, and even the gang-bangers seem to take notice and respect how some favorable attention was being brought into the area by these artistic efforts—so much so that the YMCA let us perform during events, and provided free lifeguard training for me and the crew. Moreover, we even helped a local martial arts instructor (Grandmaster Gregory Jaco) and an African drummer group set-up their schools.

Whether it was Ms. Cynthia McKinney of the

Parkways community center, teachers at Parkside, or peers from the neighborhood, having a strong sense of pride in myself and those in my area were not lost concepts.

While enjoying the fruits of success from creative arts, a change in my mother's health condition led to her having two nervous breakdowns within three years, and, my having to relocate to Aunt Juanita Kemp's apartment on 1028 East Hyde Park Boulevard.

The orderly and commercially developed community with banks, shopping centers, beaches and the University of Chicago was entirely different from my old neighborhood; moreover, although she was an elder who was a retired teacher of the Chicago Public Schools, there was one critical continuum–she loved me too.

Her love became evident when my stepfather Lonnie Blackman Sr. had died—despite the fact that she refused to let me attend the funeral. It was an event that equated to having the only world known to me at the time being crushed.

During the seven years that followed, she wisely nurtured the century old family traditions that my grandmother and she had taught my mother who in turn had taught me.

We attended many fine arts performances by legends like Yul Brenner and Sammie Davis Jr. at the Arie Crown Theatre or McCormick Place; visited the farmlands in Cassopolis, Michigan; and celebrated the annual Easter Teas hosted by the Kemp family's Good Shepherd Congregational Church.

She would enroll me in a private elementary school-- DeLena Day School—once owned and operated by an official of the Congregational Church community by the name of Bishop William Moore.

She introduced me to gardening on the family's Chicago property, banking by opening a savings account for me, and negotiations with renters of the family's farmlands in Cassopolis, Michigan.

Learning about refined arts, handling legal or financial affairs, agricultural development, civic and church service, as well as, obtaining a quality independent education, the lessons she was teaching me were fostering those family norms that extended way back from Alabama post Emancipation and beyond.

While teachers at DeLena School—like Mrs. Walton—reminded me about the history of Marcus Garvey and the meanings of the red, black and green flag, my aunt made sure that critical subjects like geography, the sciences, reading literacy, math, as well as, the Illinois and United States Constitutions were known to me.

As a matter-of-fact, any comfort or ease with my present studying of constitutional law directly extends from her mastery at preparing me and other students for society—a double dose of genuine love from her passion for family and commitment to the teaching profession.

While this season of my life seemed to be in an upswing, hindsight has revealed that as sure as the sun was rising on our time the "sun was setting" on our predecessor's era because the champion torchbearer of our family's traditions—my uncle James H. Kemp, Jr.—died.

His death seemed particularly surreal because we were just celebrating his election to the presidency of the NAACP. Having been appointed near the beginning of the year, the church's annual Easter Tea of 1983 was electrified as "Uncle Jimmy" gracefully entered the affair to the cheers of the proud community. Despite the hole his absence left in the family—and in turn, my Great Aunt Nita—his "home-going" celebration seemed energized by the string of city, state, religious, and labor dignitaries in attendance. Even in the midst of the social spectacular, my Aunt Juanita Kemp intuitively positioned me front and center of the action, thus, making sure that my place and position as a progenitor of the illustrious Kemp legacy was known to all.

While changing my social exposure and environment did produce desirable results, however, my transition from the dilapidated apartments in the pre-gentrified neighborhood of sixty-seventh and Stoney Island into the upper middle class Hyde Park community was not without a few bumps.

The intimacy of a private elementary school had to be shed for the more crowded and faster public high school life of Kenwood Academy. Those shifts in academic and social settings were the first real tests of my realigned adolescence—ultimately, my handling of those changes lead to floundering results at best.

Although my grades and social standings slightly suffered, my great Aunt Nita was not going to risk my falling behind or sliding completely out of academic bounds; therefore, several months after my prayers for a "fresh start" had preceded her "firm" choice, she made the decision to move me to the far south Chicago suburbs in order to complete my high school education.

It is said that if you love someone, then, let them go and see if they return. The tears and words of encouragement from my Great-Aunt Juanita Kemp confirmed her love for me; thus, it was accompanied by my promise to graduate from high school and to "do good". My choice was simple: shun any activity that would threaten my ability to graduate from high school and prevent me from flying back to my nest of love in Chicago.

Never was it my suspicion that the move to Sauk Village, Illinois in the summer of 1987 was the beginning to an awesome transformation in my life.

Although my prayers to God was for a new beginning, it wasn't long before the walking of country miles and small town rural surroundings made me ask: "Lord why did you send me to this place"! Nevertheless, and contrary to my culture shock, my relocating into the Johnson family was a done deal, so, there was simply no turning back.; moreover, Mr. and Mrs. Johnson were not completely new to our family. Following their adoption of my three younger siblings, my visitation with Warren and Mildred Johnson had began as far back as the early 1980s. There was a time span of several years from my visiting their home in Ford Heights, Illinois and Momma Millie (as we affectionately call her) coming to our Hyde Park home prior to 1987. So, in retrospect, moving from Chicago was another one of my Aunt Juanita's well-orchestrated expressions of love.

It was during this summer of change that my journey through Bloom Trail High School began. It was appropriate that the school's mascot was the "Trailblazers" since a new trail for my life would become ablazed in academic, sports, and inter-scholastic clubs. Many committed teachers at Bloom Trail influenced me, however, the one educator who simply refused to let me fade into the background or tolerate less than my best was Mrs. Emily Means-Willis. A stern-spirited woman from Tennessee, Mrs. Willis insisted on me joining the honor's English classes, and seeking the presidency of Bloom Trail's African-American Society—the latter of which was the farthest from my desire, thus, my choice for the job were two popular youth from Ford Heights with me at public relations (she reluctantly accepted).

Ducking the bullet of a high-profile student political office, and although unknown to me, the struggle for my intellectual soul with Mrs. Willis was far from over. Countering her fervor for motivating me into a leadership position was my equally fervent urban survival tactic of fading to the background and not drawing too much attention. However, seemingly determined to get me into some kind of spotlight, her next plan was to insist on me taking an oratory slot in the Academic, Cultural, Technological and Scientific Olympics of the NAACP (referred to as the ACT-SO competitions).

Ultimately, her insistence on my participation in the competition proved correct and rewarding for myself and for the school's image. My victory at the local competition with a speech from a popular south-side Chicago Congregational Church minister[1] brought some good public relations for Mrs. Willis, the NAACP's local branch, my school peers, and the high school.

The culmination of my psychological clash with Mrs. Willis was an event that would officially usher me into academic scholarship, and, realign me with another century old family tradition—Bloom Trail's first Historical Black College Tour through Tennessee and Georgia.

During this period of personal and academic growth, two other teachers—Mrs. Cleveland and Mrs. Gress—made some noteworthy impacts on my collegiate preparation. Mrs. Gress was the teacher of the CAP-I Prep course which provided me with several life skill tips: make long-term decisions for life beyond high school instead of allowing life's basic activities to sidetrack or derail collegiate ambitions (i.e. marriage, having children, and living expenses); also, she placed great emphasis on making resumes, vocabulary building, and working with those interested in the collective good of America's citizens, a healthy dose of humanism.

If Mrs. Willis was my chief influence on African-American pride, integrity, and societal significance, then, Mrs. Cleveland could be considered the influence for the rest of the American multi-ethnic groups due to her exposing me to the cultural influences of great Italian restaurants and educational trips to the University of Chicago. The activity became a pivotal benchmark for my academic transformation when a former home room teacher from Kenwood Academy stood in amazement upon my being among the same group as his current "college-bound students". It was Mrs. Cleveland, along with Mrs. Willis, who wrote my recommendation letters for college admission. Ultimately, these three teachers would collectively leave a humanitarian impression on my overall view of American society.

My academic fate was sealed following the visits to the campuses of several HBCUs or Historical Black Colleges and Universities: Fisk University, Tennessee State University, and the Atlanta University Center schools of Morehouse, Spellman, Morris Brown, and Clark Atlanta University. The flurry of intellectual jabs from

Mrs. Willis's academic activities delivered a knockout to my ideals that could rival punches thrown by heavy weight champs Joe Louis, Muhammad Ali, and Mike Tyson. My acceptance into Clark Atlanta University, Columbia College of Chicago, and Bauder College for Broadcasting in Florida signaled the success of my Aunt Juanita Kemp's gambit, as well as, my assumption of the Kemp family's academic mantle and community service.

Although my options for attending college were vast, the period from the mid 1980s into 1990s was a season for heightened discussions about "Afro-centric" thought or "black talk". Following my whirlwind visit to many HBCUs—and since Emerge magazine ranked Clark Atlanta University as the number one college for black awareness—my journey into the Atlanta University Center seemed like the fulfillment of destiny; moreover, the family matriarch—my Great Aunt Juanita Kemp—was so ecstatic over the "prodigal son's" return to the family's traditional folds that she couldn't stop telling all of her retired educator friends how proud she was of my victories at the NAACP, choice of college, and "political talk".

Fully excited by the future prospects of college and life, my Aunt Nita entrusted me with a family heirloom that she was preparing to include in a collection of gifts for the DuSable Museum—a century old hand made scrapbook of "Negro" history. The compilation of historical documents consisted of original news articles, words of Booker T. Washington[2], W.E.B. DuBois discussions[3], Jubliee Songs[4], poems of Paul Laurence Dunbar[5], interviews of Elijah Muhammad[6] and Malcolm X[7], and various statistics about the evolution of the Negro Race in America[8]. Making this gesture of a gift was the single act of generosity from my Aunt Nita to make clear of her intentions and trust for me to embody and pass on a family legacy that was literally thought-out, assembled, handwritten, and bound in book form by my grandmother Marjorie Kemp and Great Aunt Juanita Kemp[9]. Since my heart, soul and mind was filled with zeal, then, my collegiate and life journey continued.

Although attending college in the Atlanta University Center had me feeling like a kid in a candy store, the non-monolithic cultural realities fueled the constant battle for the "head negro in charge" crown of black idealistic supremacy.

Despite the propaganda and hyper-spin about black consciousness and black unity it became obvious to me—after touring the philosophical afro circus—that it was practically counterproductive for too many idealism to be vying for the attention of the twelve thousand plus college student body of the AUC. Actually, in essence, it was more like a popular intellectual mall, swap meet, or bazaar!

An overload of ideals were advanced by the usual

Greek letter organizations, the civil rights cast of Rev. Dr. Martin Luther King, W. E. B. DuBois, or the afro-centric doctrines of Dr. Ben Jochanan, Anthony Browder, J.A. Rogers, Haki Mahabutti, and Dr. Francis Cress Welsing. Also present were the concepts of Black Nationalistic thought by Maulana Karenga, the Shrine of The Black Madonna Christian Church, an Ancient Egyptian Fraternity, and various offshoot branches from members of the original Nation of Islam (Elijah Muhammad, Silis Muhammad, Louis Farrakhan, Warith Muhammad, Imam Isa, Nubians, Clarence 13 X, etc).

My time in Atlanta's academic labs culminated with a set of business skills that were enabling me to develop the concepts for a social service entity (Tyllman Enterprises NFP) and an entertainment entity (later named The MO Amper, LLC).

The cultural and intellectual offerings from the all-you-can eat buffet of "black-talk" were fascinating to engage, however, after years of college classes, restaurant management and a Million Man March, the core of my being was calling out for the original purpose for coming to college—music business.

My intellect and soul was yearning for mass communications, entertainment, and community or social services.

Following a three-year tour of the AUC and the Atlanta Metropolitan Technical College complexes, my collegiate and restaurant managerial experiences were packed up with a few personal belongings and return-shipped back to the real-world streets of Chicago in 1996.

It was away from the small town surroundings of HBCU academia in Atlanta that my life's work and calling towards the Kemp family traditions began to take shape.

Developing the intellectual and creative abilities of young people was an outgrowth from the Kemp family's journey after Emancipation, which fostered my budding "social service" leanings, while teaching my junior high peer—Laurence McKinney (aka-"Dinky")—some basics in reading literacy at De Lena Day School.

However, while my stimulus for social service happened in my youth, the shaping of my professional craft as an educator was by direct mentorship from the executives of the F.U.T.U.R.E. Foundation.

Upon returning to Chicago, my focus was on formalizing my business concepts, completing my career training at Columbia College, and applying my new skills in the work force. All three of these goals were achieved by 1999. My personal goals on track, the stage was set for my emersion into the struggles between the proverbial haves and have-nots, thus, my acceptance of Emir Hardy's offer to create and launch a youth training program at his center located in the "poorest suburb of America"[9]—Ford Heights, Illinois. Since my time in high school, Emir's F.U.T.U.R.E. Foundation sparked my interests in Africultural and martial arts like Copeira and Tai Chi Chuan[10] (taught by Master Tolo-Naa, aka, Ray Cooper Sr.). F.U.T.U.R.E. was the ideal place to launch my social programs for youth.

By the summer of 1999, some of my college-level training was distilled into my arts program—Musical Minds. The initiative was launched due to the initial financial and business support from Emir and the foundation's co-director—Theresa Kennedy-Patton[11]. My entertainment networks from performance venues like Some Like It Black coffee house, Salaam Restaurant, and the House of Blues, were pivotal to garnering the support for exposing the program in major radio, print media, and music business arenas like Billboard magazine[12].

More proof in my life that the Kemp family tradition of educating our future leaders had come full-circle was the subsequent college graduation of one of the program's youth who was also creating college chapters for the Alpha Phi Alpha fraternity (personally significant since the men of Alpha Phi Alpha attempted to recruit me during my years at Clark Atlanta University).

Although my direct tenure at the F.U.T.U.R.E. foundation would change due to the ever-shifting impact of social service funding in 2001, my sense of mission and family tradition did not subside. My Musical Minds program was brought under the now incorporated Tyllman Enterprises Not-for-Profit and contracted to organizations like the Abraham Lincoln Center, Lakeside Community Center, and Cabrini Green tutoring program headed by Theresa Kennedy-Patton.

While completing my Columbia College training, an opportunity arose for me to teach a music program at the Gallery 37 complex operated by the mayor's wife in downtown Chicago[13]. The well-financed and equipped facility was a clear example of "the haves" and a direct contrast to the "have-nots" economically impoverished communities of Cabrini Green, Bronzeville, and Ford Heights—a lesson that has never been lost on me.

The experience at Gallery 37 affirmed for me the necessity for advocating youth education, resource accessibility, and the application of technology. Since the inception of my tenure in providing social services to youth, the programs always incorporated a hands-on component with the latest in digital technology. For example, the television production studios and radio station WCSU at Chicago State University (formerly Chicago Normal School) was where the Musical Minds youth participants were trained in 2000; where my first radio program was contracted by the World Space International Satellite Radio service (now part of XM radio) in 2001; and, the gateway where my multi-media alliances with Russell Simmon's & Bruce George's DEF Poetry would launch in 2001 until 2008[14]; Furthermore, as the institution where my Great Aunt Juanita Kemp and

Grandfather Henry Spaulding graduated in the early 1920s[15], it was another continuum of academic and cultural family traditions.

The digital and social divide in accessing resources motivated me to expose youth to the equipment, as well as, the colleges and actual professional venues of my life. Thus, the places where my entertainment products were manufactured and featured—bookstores, coffee houses, radio stations, recording studios, colleges, etc.—became the educational platforms for the youth's training[16].

In order to bridge the technological divide in resources and offset some of the expenses to my social service partners, a partnership was formed with the Digital Media Center of the Illinois Institute of Technology in 2001. During this four-year relationship, my use of the power of freedom afforded by the media and arts enabled me to enter into the international forum for human rights.

Issues like the unfair labor practices as championed by the Coalition of the Immokalee Workers for the Mexican-American tomato pickers in Florida; the human rights violations of proponents of Falon-Gong in Asia; the international nuclear energy awareness; and concerns about the violation of American civil liberties under the Patriot Act's counter-terrorism policies—specifically, the labeling of youths and entertainers as "domestic terrorist".

Many of the results from this digital technology, arts and entertainment alliances included the funding of high school and college youth to create my company's web sites; organizing events for bridging the digital divide at Chicago area businesses; networking with interfaith religious and civic leaders during the Millions More Movement; as well as, creating the two part film series *Leaders: Gangs, Guerillas, Gods or Hip-Hop Terrorists*—the films were screened at various colleges in Chicago, and featured at the 2007 International Hip-Hop Film Festival in New York City[17].

When considering that the Illinois Institute of Technology was where my uncle James H. Kemp graduated from when it went by the name Lewis University in the 1930s[18], and, where my wife and I met in 2005, the fruit of this relationship was thrice as sweet.

Since moving to my wife's hometown in South Carolina over seven years ago, many events have ushered in another cycle of an African-based tradition called the rites of passage—my 'marriage and teacher phase'—a phase occurring after marriage or by thirty-three years of age in my case[19]. There was the establishment of a music publishing agency for administrating intellectual property or copyrights featured in music recordings—the first success appropriately performed by Talib Kweli and Hi-Tec in 2008[20] (Ballad of the Black Gold); a college student organization at Greenville Technical College in 2009—Cr.A.F.T. (an acronym meaning Creative Artist Focused on Training)[21]; the completion of my Master's Degree for Entertainment Business Management in 2011, and acceptance into Charlotte School of Law in 2012.

However, no event has been more significant in my assumption of the teacher phase of life than the arrival of my first-born child—Royce Felder-Commander, and, my first daughter—Rayna Grace Aria Commander.

The birth of my children have set in motion the wheels of time on a cycle of life that has intensified the need for me to provide a more exemplary service for humanity. Perhaps this sense of purpose revolves around an obligation to uphold what have been traditions in my American-based family for over one hundred and fifty years; Maybe the desire for trailblazing a clear path for the next generations under my watch steams from the evident reality of my children's evolution.

Nevertheless, whether the need to assume my role stems from the ways of my ancestors, or the responsibility of stewardship, the most critical motivation and power for accomplishing any of the aforementioned tasks is the same force of soul that has driven generations before me—the love at our roots.

(Left Photo) James H. Commander graduating from the kindergarten at Parkside School. (Right photo) The De Lena Day School in the Hyde Park neighborhood of Chicago.

(Bottom left photo) Diploma from De Lena School in 1985. (Bottom right photo) James H. Commander graduating from 8th grade at De Lena.

(Photo) 1983 brochure listing of how the Kemp family contributes to secure the Wicks American Classical Organ as their support for the Good Shepherd Congregational Church continues.

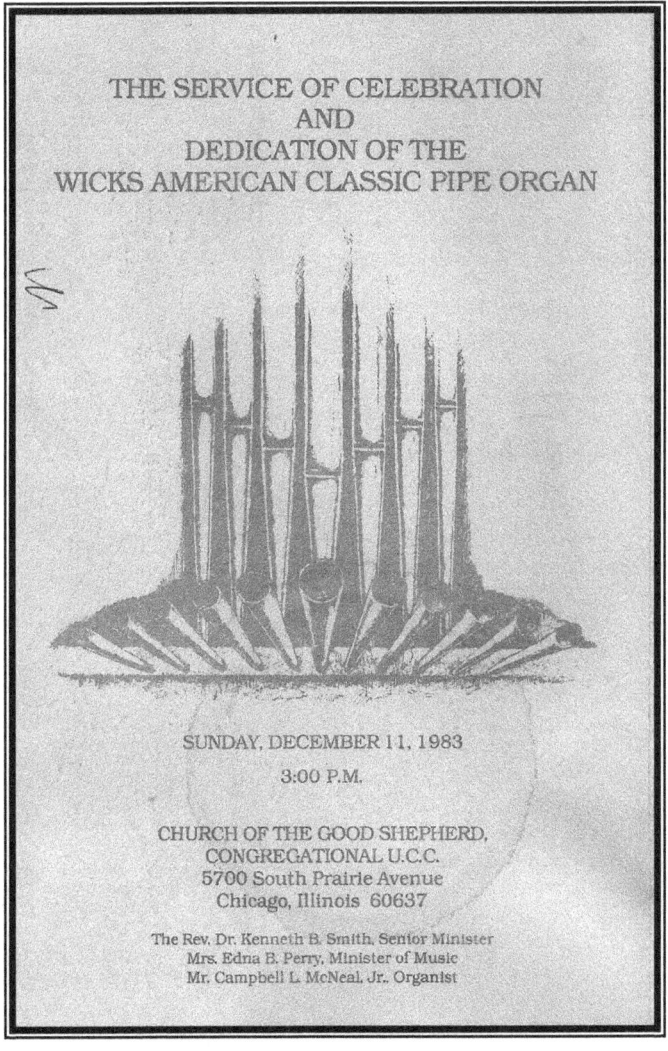

THE SERVICE OF CELEBRATION
AND
DEDICATION OF THE
WICKS AMERICAN CLASSIC PIPE ORGAN

SUNDAY, DECEMBER 11, 1983
3:00 P.M.

CHURCH OF THE GOOD SHEPHERD,
CONGREGATIONAL U.C.C.
5700 South Prairie Avenue
Chicago, Illinois 60637

The Rev. Dr. Kenneth B. Smith, Senior Minister
Mrs. Edna B. Perry, Minister of Music
Mr. Campbell L. McNeal, Jr., Organist

Dedication
of the

James Kemp
Locomotive

June 12, 1985

LaSalle Street Station
Chicago, Illinois

(Left photo) Brochure dedicating the train #105 as the "James H. Kemp." Dedication by Rapid Transit Authority of Chicago, Illinois.

(Right photo) The Metra train #105 — the James H. Kemp is still in service for travel through Chicago, Illinois.

In Loving Memory Of

James Horace Kemp

The Helm Family

(Left photo) An ad page for James Horace Kemp from his daughter's family placed in the annual Easter Tea book of the Good Shepherd Congregational Church in Chicago, Illinois.

(Left photo) An ad page for Juanita Kemp in the Easter Tea book of the Good Shepherd Congregational Church in Chicago, Illinois.

(Bottom photo) Ad page for Marjorie Kemp-Spaulding, her daughter Pamela, and nine grandchildren in 1986.

Compliments

to

Juanita Kemp

Mr. & Mrs. Edward Kemp

In Loving Memory

Marjory Kemp Spaulding

Mother – Grandmother

Pamela	Terri	Maurice
Angela	James	Tawanda
Doris	Lonnie	Kemp

(Top Left photo) James H. Commander in Hyde Park Chicago circa 1987. (Bottom right photo) James H. Commander in bottom center picture at the Atlanta University Center during the historical Black College and University Tour in 1990. Later that year he would enroll in Clark Atlanta University.

(Top Left photo) James H. Commander with wife Rosemerry at the Park Manor Christian Church in Chicago with pastors, sorority members, and community activists organizing for the Millions More Movement in 2005.

(Above photo) James H. Commander with wife for presentation of my documentary film 'The Leaders: Gangs, Guerillas, Gods or Hip-Hop Terrorists' with international filmmakers, and celebrities for the International Hip-Hop Film Festival in New York in 2007.

(Right photo) Graduation from Columbia College of Chicago, with wife, Rosemerry Commander.

(Mid Photo) Rosemerry Felder-Commander accepted into South Carolina Bar.

(Right photo) Charlotte School of Law with son Royce Felder-Commander.

(Right photo) Charleston Law students pose with Dr. Cornell West.

EPILOGUE

The idea of Love has an endless amount of explanation and definitions. During the writing of this book, the five quotes at the introduction of each chapter were to serve as guiding principles or parameters for each section's subject matter. Moreover, the concept within each quote seemed to encapsulate a very broad and specific ideal for serious consideration while reading the chapter's content—as well as the chapters that followed. The following is my attempt to clarify the use of each quote as it pertains to the historical and future significance of its meaning for this book.

CHAPTER 1 – A PATCH OF BLUE: 1889-1922

"It is a gray day."
"Yes, but dinna ye see the patch of blue?"
-Scotch Shoemaker-

How appropriate is the idea of seeing a clear path in a seemingly dark condition? Cicero Kemp along with his first and second wife Anaca and Aria were born into an area of America known as 'the black belt'. According to Ira Berlin's account in *The Making of African America: The Four Great Migrations*, the area in the state of Alabama with the most concentration of slaves was the black belt; moreover, this area was full of unfamiliar lands and very unlikely to inspire the desire to "escape slavery". However, the ancestors of the Kemp family living in this period of time saw the "patch of blue" in these grey conditions. Although farm laborers (which was another term for slave hand or field slave) during the mid 1800s before President Lincoln's "Emancipation Proclamation" of 1867, the Kemp family DID NOT ACCEPT such terms of limitations. Contrary to the legal and social realities under which they lived, they chose to follow the industrial changes and opportunities being offered in a changing and evolving America. Embracing the idea of freedom, and despite the "grey" clouds of opposition, they chose to pursue "the patch of blue" in spiritual, economic, educational, and social advancement. A way was paved for their children to fly in the blue skies of opportunities for which they themselves never had a chance to enjoy.

CHAPTER 2 – A MIRACLE OF THE GOOD SHEPHERD: 1922-1944

> "Pray for powers equal to your tasks.
> Then the doing of your work shall be no miracle,
> But you shall be a miracle."
> -Phillips Brooks-

The quote specifically addresses the empowerment of one's self in order to reach personal goals. The accomplishments of the Kemp family during the period of being farm laborers or coal miners, students of academia, and founders at the Good Shepherd Congregational Church during most of the twentieth century WAS NOT coincidental. Their sincerity for freedom was facilitated by a supporting group of people and organizations like family members, church community, American Missionary Association, Crisis Magazine of the N.A.A.C.P., and local social and civic leaders from Alabama. It is important to note how there was an interwoven continuum for freedom from their existence under the legalization of slavery in America; commitment under the industrialized Jim Crow era after the emancipation proclamation; dedication to formal education via emerging Normal Schools and Colleges, as well as, social strivings for achievements in the face of civil roadblocks. If there was one thing for certain throughout their sojourn from the southern states into the mid-western states of America, then, it was their unswerving faith in God that enabled them to persevere. It is vital to understand the amount of preparation, as well as, the measure of patience they required in order to obtain their objectives. They diligently worked—as well as prayed-- for over a century, thus, the transformation of themselves and their reality became the proof of God's ability to work miracles.

CHAPTER 3 – STAGGERED NOT AT THE PROMISE: 1922-1950

> "We took so much for granted
> but we worked hard for our freedom...
> ...we felt ourselves to be the New Negro"
> -Katherine Dunham
> (Legendary Renaissance Icon, 1907-2007)

> "Negritude! Negritude is beautiful!"
> -Francis Taylor-Dunham-Catlett
> (Legendary Renaissance Icon, Age 102)

What better way to demonstrate how a person STAGGERRED NOT at the promise then to declare that "we felt OURSELVES TO BE" the promise itself? The demonstration of being a teacher, labor leader, church or school founder, social service trailblazer, and family nurturer was how members of the Kemp family revealed their inner most beliefs. Another way of stating this principle is that actions speak louder than words! Their actions bore testimony to the fact that "WE WORKED HARD FOR OUR FREEDOM". Despite what may have seemed like the prevailing opinions of many in the local and national society, the Kemp's view of their own significance was an unending declaration of WHO WE ARE IS BEAUTIFUL. Defining their own self worth in the midst of ill-spirited and mischievous mischaracterizations was how they forged a well polished iron will of determination for showing themselves and the world how to define them. Ultimately, they not only staggered not at the promise, but, they staggered not at who they understood themselves to be.

■■■

CHAPTER 4 - ENDURE ALL THINGS: 1950-1975

> "I endure all things for the sake of God's own people;
> so that they also may obtain salvation...
> and with it eternal glory."
> -2 Timothy. 2:10-
> BIBLE [KJV]

The Kemp family fostered a sense of sacrificial leadership for themselves and communities at large because it was critical "so that they ALSO"—present and future generations-- may achieve an ever-improving existence. A formal education and a career opportunity could provide a greater degree of personal benefit, however, more security for their descendents was a worthwhile goal to pursue; therefore, the Kemp family's will for enduring the various social hurdles inside the civil rights movement as well as the local and federal governments was an empowering example—also an enduring testimony and roadmap. OBTAINING the necessities for life and legacy, they developed the wherewithal to erect a lifetime of personal and public standards. Hopefully, now that clear paths have been made, their good works will serve as guides for generations that follow behind them.

CHAPTER 5 – TO WHOM MUCH IS GIVEN: 1975-The Present

"You are stronger than you think!"
-Momma Pam-

If I have the gift of prophecy and can fathom all mysteries and all knowledge, and if I have a faith that can move mountains, but do not have love, I am nothing. Love is patient, love is kind.
1 Corinthians 13:2 and 13:4 [NIV}

"You've got the world in your hands – don't drop it!"
-Aunt Patricia Spaulding-Muhammad-

The quotes for this chapter were significant because they came from my mother, biblical guidance, and a co-beneficiary from the fourth generation of Kemps. Although, my mother and aunt were siblings with "THE WORLD" in their hands, the question is which world is in their hands? Since understanding what is being held is a prerequisite to gaining insight into knowing how to

■■

handle what is possessed, then, the elders had to leave something to clarify *their world*—their WORKS! Amazingly, the family heirlooms, public documentation, civic awards, social contributions, religious and community movements are like signs posted along the highway of our life's journey. Similarly, unless we know what to look for during our travels, then, we are more than likely to miss a junction, go in the wrong direction or be on the wrong track. Also, we may not even understand what has ALREADY been created for us so that reinventing the wheel isn't necessary. In other words, we can merely pick up the torch and start running from where previous generations ended. Moreover, how can we gain our bearing when lost if we don't know the starting points? Whether gaining our center, carrying forward previous works, or staying on the right course for life, once we can identify what our hands are holding, then, we more fully realize what is in our possession. The Kemp family's force from freedom was used to construct over one hundred and sixty years of a reality or A WORLD--so that we "DON'T DROP IT"!

■■

NOTES
CHAPTER ONE: A Patch of Blue (1889-1922)
1) 'Introduction & The Origins of the Black Middle Class'; Our Kind of People: Inside America's Black Middle Class; Lawrence Otis Graham; pp. xi-18.
2) US Federal Census of 1880 and 1900.
3) World War I Draft Card of great uncle Joseph Rufus Kemp; United States, Selective Service System. *World War I Selective Service System Draft Registration Cards, 1917-1918.* Washington, D.C.: National Archives and Records Administration.; Registration State: *Alabama*; Registration County: *Walker*; Roll: *1473282.*]
4) Cudjo Lewis; http://www.encyclopediaofalabama.org/face/Article.jsp?id=h-1403
5) 'Introduction & The Origins of the Black Middle Class'; Our Kind of People: Inside America's Black Middle Class; Lawrence Otis Graham; pp. xi-18.
6) The Timetables of African-American History: A Chronology of The Most Important People and Events in African-American History; Sharon Harley.
7) 'Launching A Social Movement'; Pullman Porters and the Rise of Protest Politics in Black America 1925-1945; Beth Tompkins Bates; pg 88.
8) Alabama Probate Court records for 1911-1916 of Cicero A. Kemp, and Louis E. Kemp.
9) A Dream that Came True: Autobiography of Arthur Harold Parker; 1870-1939; pp. 11-12.
10) US Federal Census of 1900; James H. Kemp listed as "at school".
11) 1908 Talladega College Student Catalog.
12) A Dream that Came True: Autobiography of Arthur Harold Parker; 1870-1939; pg. 35
13) Alabama Probate Court records for 1911-1916 of Cicero A. Kemp, and Louis E. Kemp.
14) Alabama Probate Court records for 1911-1916 of Cicero A. Kemp, and Louis E. Kemp.
15) City Directory for Birmingham, Alabama 1916-1918.
16) A Dream that Came True: Autobiography of Arthur Harold Parker; 1870-1939; pp. 11-12.

17) <u>A Dream that Came True</u>: Autobiography of Arthur Harold Parker; 1870-1939; pp. 11-12.

CHAPTER TWO: A Miracle of The Good Shepherd (1922-1944)
1) <u>A Dream that Came True</u>: Autobiography of Arthur Harold Parker; 1870-1939; pp. 71.
2) Data of US Federal Consensus 1900, 1910, 1920, and 1930.
3) Maida Springer: Pan-Africanist and International Labor Leader; Yvette Richards
4) <u>A Dream that Came True</u>: Autobiography of Arthur Harold Parker; 1870-1939; pp. 53,63.
5) Cube Theatre playbill 1929 [front side]. [Courtesy of James Commander]
6) Photo of "Dreamy Kid" by Eugene O'Neil in debut of Four Negro Plays at The Cube Theatre. (in photo: Bertha M. Lewis, Francis Taylor Dunham-Catlett, Brunetta Barnett, and Isaac Clarke]; Chicago Daily News archives.
7) Photo of "The Man Who Died At twelve O'clock" by Paul Green in Catherine Dunham's first ever theater performance of Four Negro Plays at The Cube Theatre. [in photo: Catherine Dunham, Merideth Caldwell, and Barefield Gordon]; Chicago Daily News Archives.
8) Cube Theatre debut show list of patrons [back of playbill].(courtesy of James Commander)
9) Biographical sketch of The Church of The Good Shepherd
10) Obituary of Juanita Kemp
11) 'The Origins of the Black Upper Class'; <u>Our Kind of People: Inside America's Black Upper Class</u>; Lawrence Otis Graham; pg 13.
12) Data of US Federal Consensus 1900, 1910, 1920, and 1930.
13) 1911 Talladega College Catalogue of Students /Marjorie Kemp of Dora listing.
14) Correspondence Letters of Marjorie Kemp and W.E.B. Dubois. (University of Massachusetts archives).
15) Obituary of James H. Kemp, Jr.
16) Maida Springer: Pan-Africanist and International Labor Leader; Yvette Richards
17) Final Report of the United States Geological survey of Nebraska and portions of the adjacent territories.
   * Talladega College

18) Blacks and The American Missionary Movement; by Clara Meritt deBoer; **http://www.ucc.org/about-us/hidden-histories/blacks-and-the-american.html**
19) American Missionary Association, Talladega College of 1890 [Library of Congress]
20) Catalogue of the Officers and Students of Talladega College; by Talladega College.
21) The Cayton Legacy; A Black Metropolis; pp.116-117

CHAPTER THREE: Staggered Not at The Promise (1922-1950)
1) 1920 U.S. Federal Census.
2) Dark Mirror of Our Lives, The Cayton Legacy; pg. 131 / The Chicago Defender, Good Shepherd Community Center/Parkway Community House; April 5, 1947; pg. 15.
3) Black Chicago's First Century; Christopher Robert Reed, pg. 391
4) Excerpt from Katherine Dunham interview with Deardra Schuller; http://www.afrocentricnews.com/afro/features_katherine_dunham.html
5) Jet Magazine, 1967, pg. 8.
6) Maida Springer: Pan-Africanist and International Labor Leader; Yvette Richards; Also Maida Kemp in a Roosevelt University interview; Institute of Labor and Industrial Relations-The University of Michigan-Wayne State University; pg 91.
7) Maida Kemp in a Roosevelt University interview; Institute of Labor and Industrial Relations-The University of Michigan-Wayne State University; pg 8.
8) Maida Kemp in a Roosevelt University interview; Institute of Labor and Industrial Relations-The University of Michigan-Wayne State University; pg 7.
9) Notable Black American Women: Book II; by Jessie Carney Smith; pg. 376.
10) Notable Black American Women: Book II; by Jessie Carney Smith; pg. 376.
11) Maida Kemp in a Roosevelt University interview; Institute of Labor and Industrial Relations-The University of Michigan-Wayne State University; pg 12.

12) Maida Kemp in a Roosevelt University interview; Institute of Labor and Industrial Relations-The University of Michigan-Wayne State University; pg 14.
13) Maida Kemp in a Roosevelt University interview; Institute of Labor and Industrial Relations-The University of Michigan-Wayne State University; pg 15.
14) Maida Kemp in a Roosevelt University interview; Institute of Labor and Industrial Relations-The University of Michigan-Wayne State University; pg 14.
15) Bio Sketch of Maida Springer-Kemp, ILGWU; pg. 109.
16) Maida Kemp in a Roosevelt University interview; Institute of Labor and Industrial Relations-The University of Michigan-Wayne State University; pg 14.
17) Maida Kemp in a Roosevelt University interview; Institute of Labor and Industrial Relations-The University of Michigan-Wayne State University; pg 92.

CHAPTER FOUR: Endure All Things (1950-1975)
1) 1920 U.S. Federal Census.
2) The Cayton Legacy; A Black Metropolis; pg.119
3) The Cayton Legacy; A Black Metropolis; pg.116
4) Jet Magazine, 1967, pg. 8.
5) Maida Springer: Pan-Africanist and International Labor Leader; Yvette Richards.
6) Maida Kemp in a Roosevelt University interview; Institute of Labor and Industrial Relations-The Uniersity of Michigan-Wayne State University; pg 12
7) Notable Black American Women: Book II; by Jessie Carney Smith; pg. 376.
8) Notable Black American Women: Book II; by Jessie Carney Smith; pg. 376.
9) 1930 and 1940 U.S. Federal Census.
10) The Cayton Legacy; A Black Metropolis; pg.118.
11) Jackson County, Iowa Marriages Early 20th Century (web)
http://iagenweb.org/jackson/Marriages/20thcentury marriagessthrut.html
12) "Bridge to Benefit Boys"; Hyde Park Herald; Feb. 3, 1960; pg. 2.
13) Jet Magazine, 1962.
14) CRISIS Magazine, October 1967; pp. 420-421.

15) Jet Magazine, Dec. 4, 1969.
16) Chicago Tribune newspaper 1974.
17) Founding of DeLena Day School; "Nursery Has Until Monday"; Hyde Park Herald; December 9, 1959.
18) Founding of DeLena Day School (web)
19) Passing of founder of DeLena Day School; JET Magazine, December 1961.
20) [Original owners sold Delena to Crocket] "HPK day Care Directors Stress Individual Development" written by Sharon Glick; Hyde Park Herald; December 21, 1977.
21) Hyde Park Herald;
22) Federation News; published by The Chicago Federation of Labor and Industrial Union Council; Vol. 82 No. 6; June 1970.
23) 1908 Talladega College Student Catalog.
24) Talladega Notes from Amistad Research Center of Talladega College; Web link:
http://www.amistadresearchcenter.org/archon/?p=creators/creator&id=93
25) 1880 U.S. Federal Census; Cicero Kemp and Anaca Kemp.
26) 1900 U.S. Federal Census; Cicero and Aria Kemp.

CHAPTER FIVE: To Whom Much Is Given (1975-Future)

1) "What Makes You So Strong" speech by Rev. Jeremiah Wright of Trinity United Congregational Church of Christ in Chicago, Illinois.
2) Negro-Historical Compilation; Scrapbook of Kemp Family
3) Id.
4) Id.
5) Id.
6) Id.
7) Id.
8) Id.
9) "The Poorest Suburb In America" by Jack Hayes; Chicago Reader; Sept. 17, 1987.
10) Martial Science Institute International – "Nganga Mfundishi Tolo-Naa"; http://msii-online.com/page5.html
11) Edutainment Concert to Cap Off Musical Minds Program; South Suburban Standard, August 5, 1999.

12) Mansion Café Is Poetry and A Lot More (Some Like It Black feature) by John Anderson of Chicago Tribune; December 2, 2003;
http://articles.chicagotribune.com/2003-12-02/news/0312020305_1_singers-poetry-basement
"Rappers Practice What They Preach" by Michelle Mitchell; Billboard Magazine, August 2, 2000
13) Gallery 37 Artists Filling Vacant Lot by Robert Davis; Chicago Tribune; July 8 1993
http://articles.chicagotribune.com/1993-07-08/news/9307080126_1_gallery-maggie-daley-students
14) Bruce George's "Bandana Republic poetry anthology; features Commander's "The Brothas Gunnin".
http://books.google.com/books/about/The_Bandana_Republic_A_Literary_Antholog.html?id=rH-lHXGLAj8C
15) Emblem Yearbook 1926 for Chicago Normal College;
http://archive.org/stream/emblem__1926chic#page/n3/mode/2up

Emblem Yearbook 1927 for Freshmen of Chicago Normal College Juanita Kemp);
http://archive.org/stream/emblem__1927chic#page/n3/mode/2up
16) Chicago Reader Music Guide and Features for August 3, 2000; http://www.chicagoreader.com/chicago/trg-music-listings/Content?oid=902958
17) "The Leaders: Gangs, Guerillas, Gods and Hip-Hop Terrorists" documentary; 2007 H2O International Hip-Hop Film Festival;
http://www.flickr.com/photos/hiphopassociation/sets/72157600320330478/?page=2
18) 1937 "The Abstract" John Marshall Law School class of 1937 Abstract for James H. Kemp;
http://www.eyearbook.com/yearbooks/John_Marshall_Law_School_Abstract_Yearbook/1937/Page_37.html
19) Africana Studies: The Five Major African Initiation Rites by Professor Manu Ampin;
http://www.manuampim.com/AfricanInitiationRites.htm

20) 'Ballad of The Black Gold" by Talib Kweli and Hi-Tec is Reflection Etermal, Peaked at #3 on Billboard Top Rap Albums of 2010; http://en.wikipedia.org/wiki/Revolutions_per_Minute_%28Reflection_Eternal_album%29
21) C.R.A.F.T. – Creative Artist Focused on Training at Greenville Technical College; Greenville, South Carolina; http://www.moamper.com/craft.html

ABOUT THE AUTHOR

JAMES H. COMMANDER is a renaissance man — writer, radio personality, teacher, "art"trepreneur, husband, and father of two children. He began sharing his passion for literature, lyrics, and life since his time as a youth on the south side of Chicago, Illinois. He has been utilizing radio programming, book publishing, copyright licensing, and music recordings over the past sixteen years for the development of the renaissance arts (poetry, music, and communications). His research skills were honed from training in law school, also, masters and bachelor degrees in entertainment media management. He utilizes his research skills to validate and expound on the oral histories told by his mother and family elders. He is the son of Pamela Commander, grandson of Marjorie Kemp (Spaulding) and Henry A. Spaulding; also, the nephew of James H. Kemp, Jr. and Maida Springer-Kemp. His mother named him after her 'favorite uncle' (James H. Kemp, Jr.) whose post law school career included being a labor leader and president of the N.A.A.C.P. The author resides in South Carolina with his family currently.

Love At Our Roots   James H. Commander

www.ingramcontent.com/pod-product-compliance
Lightning Source LLC
Chambersburg PA
CBHW020005050426
42450CB00005B/327